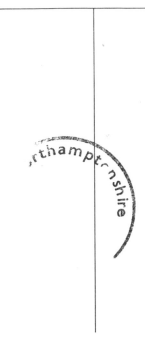 

BELIEFS AND CULTURES

Hindu

Anita Ganeri

Watts Books

London New York Sydney

© 1996 Watts Books

Watts Books
96 Leonard Street
London
EC2A 4RH

Franklin Watts Australia
14 Mars Road
Lane Cove
NSW 2066

0 7496 2060 9

10 9 8 7 6 5 4 3 2 1

Dewey Decimal Classification Number 294.5

A CIP catalogue record for this book is available
from the British Library.

Series Editor: Sarah Ridley
Designer: Liz Black
Copy Editor: Nicola Barber
Consultant: Geoff Teece
Illustrators: pages 20-21 Piers Harper; pages 5
and 22 Aziz Khan
Picture Researchers: Brooks Krikler Research
Photographer (activities): Steve Shott

Photographs: Eye Ubiquitous 12b, 24, 29b, 30b;
Robert Harding Picture Library cover (left), 14t,
22; Michael Holford 5; Hutchison Library 25l,
30t; Bipinchandra Mistry 4t, 4b, 7, 11t, 11b,
14b, 16b, 18, 19, 28, 29t; Bury Peerless 6, 25r;
Frank Spooner Picture Library 23; Trip cover
(right), 8t, 8b, 10, 12t, 15t, 15b, 16t.

Printed in Great Britain

CONTENTS

WHAT IS HINDUISM?   4

HINDU BELIEFS   6

GODS AND GODDESSES   10

WAYS OF WORSHIP   14

HOLY BOOKS AND SACRED STORIES   18

PILGRIMS AND HOLY PLACES   22

FESTIVALS   24

FAMILY CELEBRATIONS   28

INDEX   32

Hinduism is one of the world's oldest living religions. It is practised by people called Hindus who live mainly in India, where Hinduism began. Religion plays an extremely important part in the lives of Hindus, governing how they live, what they eat and how they view the world. In fact, Hindus do not call their religion 'Hinduism'. This was a term invented by Western scholars in the 19th century. Hindus simply consider their faith to be *sanatana dharma*, the 'eternal teaching' or 'eternal law'. Hinduism is a lively, colourful, flexible faith, with many ways of worship and observance.

People gather in the temple to worship, make their offerings to the gods, consult the priests and to meet friends.

This is the sacred sound 'OM', the symbol of goodness. It is often chanted to help people as they meditate.

HINDU BEGINNINGS

Hinduism is an unusual religion in having no founder nor single sacred book. It began about 4,000 years ago at the time of the Indus Valley civilisation in north-west India. Archaeologists have found Indus statues which may show an early form of the great Hindu god, Shiva. In about 1,500 BC, people from central Asia, called Aryans, invaded northern India. They brought with them their own religious beliefs, and their ideas mixed with those of the people of the Indus Valley. Hindus still worship some of the Aryan gods, such as Agni, god of fire and still read Aryan sacred texts, such as the *Rig Veda* (see page 18).

These ancient temples stand on the seashore at Mahabalipuram in South India. They are dedicated to Shiva.

Today, most Hindus live in India, but there are large Hindu communities in Nepal, the Middle East, Fiji and Mauritius. Other Hindus live and work in parts of the world such as Britain, North America, Africa, South-East Asia and the Caribbean.

Hinduism began in India but has spread to many other parts of the world, - wherever Hindus have settled.

SPOTLIGHT

- About eight out of ten of the people in India are Hindus.

- There are some 700 million Hindus worldwide.

- You have to be born a Hindu. You cannot become one.

HINDU POPULATION
- over 600 million
- 1 to 20 million
- 100,000 to 1 million
- 5,000 to 100,000

HINDU BELIEFS

Hinduism is a whole way of living, rather than a separate, formal set of religious beliefs. It can be practised in many different ways. Some Hindus pray every day; others hardly pray at all. Saying prayers and visiting the temple are not compulsory parts of Hinduism. It is left up to each individual person to decide what is best for him or her. However, all Hindus share the same basic beliefs.

Hindus believe that, when you die, your soul lives on and is reborn in another body, human or animal. This cycle of death and rebirth is called *samsara*. The quality of your next life depends on how you behave in this life. If you live a good life, you will be reborn in a higher form. If you live a bad life, you will be reborn in a lower form. This chain of actions and their effects is called *karma*.

Each village has its own small temple or shrine. It is often very simple, like this shrine underneath a tree. Villagers stop to worship here as they go about their daily lives.

The ultimate aim of a Hindu's life is to gain *moksha*, or salvation, and break free of the cycle of *samsara*. The better each rebirth, the closer to *moksha* you get. Moksha is also seen as the time when your individual soul, *atman*, merges into the supreme spirit, Brahman.

These children are studying at a religious school, called an *ashram*. They are Brahmins from the highest Hindu caste.

THE CASTE SYSTEM

Hindu society has traditionally been divided into four groups, called castes. These are Brahmins (priests), Kshatriyas (nobles and soldiers), Vaishyas (traders) and Sudras (servants). Outside the caste system are people who do jobs considered dirty or menial, such as sweeping the streets. They used to be called 'untouchables' but are now known as the 'scheduled castes'. In the past, the caste system was closely followed and people of high and low castes never mixed. Today, it is less strict but still affects where people live, what jobs they do and whom they marry.

INTERVIEW
The caste system does not really affect our lives in Britain. Traditional parents still try to find someone of the same caste for their daughter or son to marry. But we do not judge people by what caste they are.
Ramesh Chatterjee, aged 55. London, England.

FOOD TASTES AND TABOOS

Many Hindus are vegetarians. They believe in the principle of non-violence, or *ahimsa*, which means not killing things to eat. A typical Hindu vegetarian meal consists of rice or *chapattis* (rounds of flat bread), several spicy vegetable dishes, *dhal* (lentils), *dahi* (yoghurt) and pickles. Hindus traditionally eat with their fingers, using their right hands.
They consider their left hands to be unclean.

On festival days, people exchange gifts of home-made sweets. The sweets are mainly made of milk, nuts and sugar.

Hindus treat cows as sacred animals and never eat beef, even if they are not strict vegetarians.

In India, cows are never harmed or killed but allowed to roam freely, even along busy, traffic-filled streets.

MAKING CARROT HALVA

YOU WILL NEED: (for 4 people)

- 450g grated carrots
- 750ml milk
- 1 tablespoon sultanas
- 4 tablespoons caster sugar
- 8 cardamom pods
- 3 tablespoons of vegetable oil
- 1 tablespoon crushed, unsalted pistachio nuts
- Thick-based saucepan
- Non-stick frying pan
- Wooden spoon
- Cream (optional)

♣ Ask an adult for help with the cooking.

NOTE: if your local supermarket does not have all these ingredients, you can get them from any Asian grocer.

WHAT TO DO:

1 Bring the carrots, cardamom pods and milk to the boil in the saucepan. Lower the heat and simmer for about an hour, or until the liquid has gone, stirring regularly.

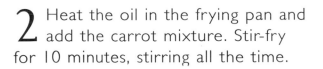

You can pick out the cardamom pods at this stage if you don't like their strong flavour.

2 Heat the oil in the frying pan and add the carrot mixture. Stir-fry for 10 minutes, stirring all the time.

3 Add the sugar, sultanas and crushed pistachio nuts. Stir-fry the mixture for another 2-3 minutes.

4 Spoon the halva into bowls and serve warm, with a spoonful of cream.

Most Hindus believe in a supreme spirit, Brahman. But Hindus do not pray to Brahman, as Christians pray to God or Muslims to Allah. Instead, they worship hundreds of gods and goddesses who represent different aspects of Brahman. Some Hindus worship many gods. Some worship one specific god. Others do not formally worship any gods at all.

Hindu gods and goddesses are often shown with many heads or arms, each holding a sacred object. These features symbolise their special powers and the aspect of Brahman that they represent.

Vishnu, the preserver and protector of the universe, and his wife, Lakshmi, the goddess of wealth and beauty.

THE HINDU TRINITY

The three most important Hindu gods are Brahma, the creator, Vishnu, the preserver and Shiva, the destroyer. Vishnu and Shiva are very popular gods, with many temples dedicated to them.

Brahma

Brahma, the first member of the Hindu trinity, is the creator of the universe. He is shown with four heads, facing each of the four corners of the earth. He rides on a swan or sits on a sacred lotus blossom. His wife is the goddess of learning and the arts, Saraswati. Brahma has four hands, one always raised in blessing.

Vishnu

Vishnu is the preserver of the universe. He is often shown riding on an eagle or sleeping on a giant serpent. His wife is Lakshmi, goddess of beauty and wealth.

This statue shows Shiva, Lord of Dance. The circle of flame round him represents the never-ending cycle of time.

knowledge. Shiva rides on a huge bull, called Nandi. His wife is the goddess Parvati.

Rama and Krishna

Rama and Krishna are worshipped as gods all over India. Rama is the hero of the *Ramayana* poem (see page 19) and represents virtue and courage. Krishna is more mischievous and fond of performing miracles. He is a key figure in the *Bhagavad Gita* which forms part of the *Mahabharata* poem (see page 19).

Shiva

Shiva is the destroyer of evil in the universe. He carries a trident, the symbol of destruction. On his forehead is the third eye of

Rama is one of the most popular of all Hindu gods. He is shown here with his wife, Sita.

SPOTLIGHT

Vishnu has visited the Earth nine times to save the world from evil in times of trouble. These are the disguises he used:
1 Matsya, the fish
2 Kurma, the tortoise
3 Varaha, the boar
4 Narasimha, the lion
5 Vamana, the dwarf
6 Parusha-Rama, the warrior
7 Rama, the ideal man
8 Krishna, the blue god
9 Buddha, the founder of Buddhism

Kalki, the 10th visit, is yet to come.

The power of the goddess

Parvati is often worshipped as the kind, gentle mother goddess. But in other forms she can be cruel and terrible. As Durga, warrior goddess, she rides a tiger and holds a weapon in each of her ten hands. As the goddess, Kali, she wears a skull necklace and conquers the ugliness of evil.

Ganesh

Ganesh, the elephant-headed god, is the son of Shiva and Parvati and one of the most popular Hindu gods. The story goes that Shiva cut off Ganesh's original human head in a rage and later replaced it with a wise elephant's head.

The gods once lent Durga their weapons and begged her to kill the terrible buffalo demon, Mahishasura.

Ganesh is worshipped as the god who removes difficulties. So Hindus pray to him whenever they start something new, such as a new job, new school or when they move house.

MAKING A GANESH ELEPHANT MASK

YOU WILL NEED:
- grey card (or white card, painted grey) • pencil
- glue   • paint   • glitter
- elastic   • scissors   • paintbrush
- sequins or tinsel   • sticky tape

WHAT TO DO:

1 Fold the card in half and draw the shape of half an elephant's head on it. Cut out and complete with ears and eyeholes. Fold the ears so they stick out slightly.

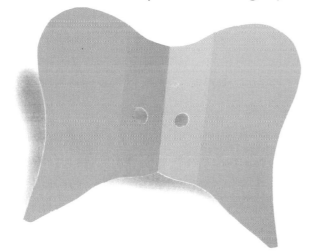

2 Cut another piece of card in the shape of the elephant's trunk. Shape the trunk slightly so that it curls to one side.

3 Stick the trunk on to the inside of the head. Then decorate the mask. Paint dots around the eyes, or stick on tinsel or sequins. Sprinkle on some glitter. Make a hole at each side of the mask by the earfolds and thread some elastic through.

Make sure the elastic is big enough to go round your head. Knot the ends through the holes.

WAYS OF WORSHIP

Hindus worship in temples, most of which are dedicated to a particular god or goddess. The temple is seen as the god's home on Earth and a statue of the god stands in the innermost, most sacred part of the temple. There is no obligation for Hindus to visit the temple or to pray regularly, although a great many Hindus make a special visit on festival days or family occasions.

There are thousands of temples in India, in every town and village. Temples have also been built in other countries where Hindus have settled.

People visit small, roadside shrines on their way to work or school. They say a short prayer or leave an offering.

In India and abroad, temples are important places for the whole community, full of noise, colour and life.

WORSHIP AT HOME

Hindus also worship at home or at roadside shrines. Many Hindu homes have a room or part of a room set aside as a shrine, with a statue or picture of the god or goddess. Here the family performs its prayers, or *puja*, in the morning and evening. You take your shoes off before you approach the shrine, just as you would in a temple.

At home, the family shrine may be a whole room, part of a room, or simply a small cupboard or a shelf.

VISITING THE TEMPLE

There are no set services in a Hindu temple, as there are in a Christian church, for example. People can visit whenever they like for puja and for *darshana*, meaning a sight of a sacred image that symbolises the presence of a god or goddess.

People must take off their shoes before entering the temple and walk clockwise round the main shrine, with their right hands towards the god. They bring offerings of fruit, sweets and flowers, called *prasada*. The temple priest lays these offerings before the god to be blessed, then returns them to the worshippers to bestow the god's blessing upon

Every Hindu temple has a bell. You ring the bell as you enter the temple and again as you leave it.

them. With his finger, the priest marks the foreheads of the people with the red *tilaka* (sign) of blessing. Worshippers also pass their hands over the sacred fire, then over their heads as a form of blessing.

Outside every temple, there are stalls selling offerings for the gods, such as sweets, incense and garlands of flowers. The garlands are hung on the statue of the god or goddess inside the temple.

INTERVIEW

I go to the temple once a week with my mother and at special times such as the Diwali and Holi festivals. I also say my prayers every day in the small shrine room in my house. I like it best when the whole family joins in the puja and my parents tell us stories about the gods.
Nidhi Churiwala, aged 13. Calcutta, India.

PRIESTS AND HOLY MEN

Each temple has its own Brahmin priest. Priests also visit people's homes to recite the sacred texts and prepare horoscopes, and to perform special ceremonies such as weddings. In return, the priests are given gifts of food and money. *Sadhus* are holy men who have given up all their worldly goods to wander from place to place in search of enlightenment and salvation.

The horizontal marks on this sadhu's forehead show he is a follower of Shiva. Sadhus who follow Vishnu have three vertical marks on their foreheads.

The different positions or postures of yoga are called *asanas*. This yogi is sitting in the lotus position.

YOGA AND MEDITATION

Some holy men, and indeed, ordinary Hindus, use yoga and meditation to concentrate their minds in their search for moksha. Yoga involves exercises for both the mind and body and has become very popular all over the world. You learn to control your body through breathing and posture and to concentrate your mind through meditation. Meditation can mean concentrating very hard on a special pattern called a *mandala*, or repeating, inwardly or out loud, a special word or phrase called a *mantra*.

MAKING A MARIGOLD GARLAND

YOU WILL NEED:

- *marigold flowers*
- *a large needle*
- *strong thread*
- *scissors*

WHAT TO DO:

1 Pinch off the marigold flower heads. You could also use roses, pinks or any other small, sturdy flowers.

2 Cut a length of thread about 120cm long. Thread the needle.

3 Push the needle through the centre of each flower head to thread them on.

4 Tie the ends of the thread with a firm knot. Your garland is now ready to wear or to offer to the god.

Hindus do not have one holy book, such as the Christian Bible, but many different sacred texts. Long before these texts were written down, they were passed on by word of mouth. The language used was Sanskrit, the language of the Aryan people (see page 4). Sanskrit is the sacred language of India and it is still studied today, although it is not spoken in everyday life.

THE VEDAS

The most ancient sacred texts are four collections of hymns, prayers, rules for rituals and sacrifices, and spells, called the *Vedas*. These were compiled by the Aryans some 3,500 years ago. The oldest and best known is the *Rig Veda*. It is still one of the most important Hindu holy books. It contains over a thousand hymns in praise of ancient gods and goddesses.

Many Hindus read and study the sacred books as part of their worship and use them as guides for how to live their lives. Priests read from the sacred books at weddings and other ceremonies.

THE UPANISHADS

The *Upanishads* were compiled some 2,500 years ago. They deal with the relationship between Brahman and the individual soul, atman (see page 7) and use stories and parables to make philosophical points. Over a hundred of the *Upanishads* have now been written down.

EPIC POEMS

Among the holy books of Hinduism are two great poems, the *Mahabharata* and the *Ramayana*.

The *Mahabharata* tells the story of two rival families, the Kauravas and Pandavas, who are fighting for control of the kingdom of Hastinapura. The most important part of the *Mahabharata* is the *Bhagavad Gita*, the 'Song of the Lord'. In it, the god, Krishna reminds Arjuna, one of the Pandavas, that a person must do their duty selflessly in order to gain salvation.

The *Ramayana* is the story of how Rama rescues his wife, Sita, from the demon king, Ravana, helped by his faithful friend, the monkey god, Hanuman. After many adventures,

This is a passage from the *Ram Charit Manas*, a very famous version of the *Ramayana* poem, carved on a temple wall.

they complete their task and Rama and Sita return in triumph to their home in Ayodhya, to be crowned king and queen.

SPOTLIGHT

- The *Puranas* are ancient Sanskrit verses about the lives of the gods, kings and saints.

- The name *Rig Veda* means 'Song of Knowledge'.

- *Sutras* are collections of sayings and snippets of information dealing with all aspects of life.

KRISHNA AND THE SERPENT KING

From an early age, Hindu children hear stories
about the adventures of Krishna, the blue
god. Here is one of them. It comes from
the *Bhagavata Purana*, a collection of
stories about Krishna's life.

Kaliya, the serpent king, lived in the
darkest depths of the River Yamuna.
He had five heads for spitting poison
and was so huge he could crush a
person to death. He had poured so much
poison into the river that any animals or
people who drank from it were killed
instantly. Now no one dared go near
the river, for fear of being
snatched by the serpent.
Something had to be done.

Krishna decided that it was up to him to save the river and his friends. So he dived into the water, climbed on to one of Kaliya's five heads and began to dance. He danced and danced until, one by one, the heads were crushed under his feet. When he got to the last head, he stopped.

"I will spare your life on one condition," he told Kaliya. "Leave the river and flee to the sea where you can do no more harm." Kaliya was so grateful to have his life spared, that he swam away as fast as he could, never to be seen again. And the river was left in peace once more.

PILGRIMS AND HOLY PLACES

Each year, millions of Hindus make pilgrimages, or *yatras*, to holy places connected with the gods or religious events. They may visit the great temples in the seven sacred cities, or *tirthas*, of India. These are Varanasi, Hardwar, Mathura, Ayodhya, Ujjain, Dwarka and Kanchipuram. Hindus do not have to make pilgrimages but many feel that it brings them closer to *moksha*.

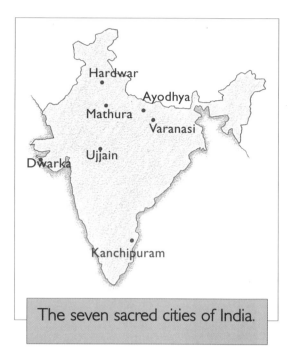

The seven sacred cities of India.

VARANASI

Varanasi is the holiest of the seven *tirthas*. The city lies on the banks of the sacred River Ganges in northern India. Hindus believe that Varanasi was chosen by Shiva as his home on Earth. Millions of pilgrims flock to Varanasi to bathe in the river and to visit the temples. Many elderly Hindus visit Varanasi because it is considered a particularly favoured place to die.

The steps leading down to the river at Varanasi are crowded with bathers, priests, temples and sacred cows.

Kumbh Mela celebrations. People bathe in the river and collect jars of sacred river water to take home with them.

THE SACRED GANGES

Hindus believe that the water of the River Ganges is sacred and that bathing in it washes away their sins. The Ganges flows from the Himalayas across northern India to the Bay of Bengal in the east. According to legend, the Ganges fell to Earth from heaven. Shiva caught the river in his hair to break its fall and prevent its weight shattering the Earth. The river is also worshipped as a goddess, called Ganga.

THE KUMBH MELA FAIR

Every 12 years, millions of pilgrims gather in the city of Allahabad. This is where the rivers Ganges and Yamuna meet the mythical Saraswati River. The actual meeting point, or *sangam*, is the site of the great Kumbh Mela fair, where people come to bathe in the waters of the holy rivers. A huge temporary town is built to accommodate the pilgrims.

SACRED MOUNTAINS

Mountains are special places, too. Mount Kailash in the Himalayas is sacred as the home of Shiva and Parvati. The Sri Amarnath cave in the Himalayas in Kashmir is also sacred to Shiva. At the time of the Full Moon in the Hindu month, Sravana (July-August: see page 26), thousands of pilgrims make the long trek to worship at the cave.

No one can escape a drenching at Holi! Students drench their teachers, children their parents - just for one day.

There are hundreds of Hindu festivals throughout the year, celebrated both in India and by Hindus living abroad. Some are national festivals; others are just local village celebrations. The celebrations may include performing puja, wearing new clothes, exchanging gifts, eating special food, singing, dancing and visiting relations.

HOLI

The colourful festival of Holi marks the welcome end of winter. On the night before Holi, bonfires are built to burn models of the witch, Holika. Legend says that Holika tried to kill her nephew because he worshipped Vishnu, but she was killed instead. On the day of Holi itself, people dress up in their old clothes and drench each other with coloured powder and water. It's great fun but very messy! In the evening, people visit their relatives with gifts of sweets. Holi is also a special festival for farmers. They celebrate gathering in the first harvest of spring.

DIWALI

Diwali is the festival of lights, and it is celebrated over five days. People decorate their houses and temples with small lamps, called *divas*. These are intended to light the hero Rama home to Ayodhya after his victory over Ravana (see page 19). There are fireworks displays in every town and village. Diwali is also dedicated to Lakshmi, the goddess of wealth, and marks the start of the Hindu New Year.

Hindus all over the world celebrate Diwali. These children in Britain are lighting the diva lamps.

At the end of the Ram Lila play, a flaming arrow is fired at the model of Ravana, setting it alight.

DUSSEHRA

The festival of Dussehra lasts for ten days. In some places, it is known as Ram Lila. Plays are performed telling the story of Rama's life, and huge models of Ravana are burnt. In other places, the festival is called Durga Puja and celebrates Durga's victory over the buffalo-headed demon, Mahishasura.

THE HINDU YEAR

The Hindu religious calendar has 12 months, based on the phases of the Moon. Each month runs from Full Moon to Full Moon and is divided into a light half and a dark half. In everyday life, Hindus use the same calendar as everyone else. The major Hindu festivals are shown below.

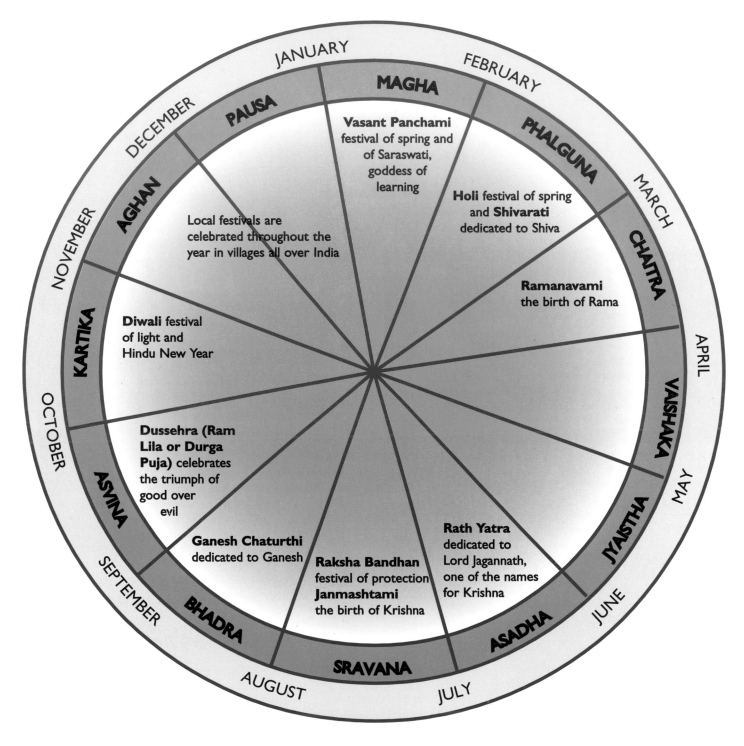

JANUARY · FEBRUARY · MARCH · APRIL · MAY · JUNE · JULY · AUGUST · SEPTEMBER · OCTOBER · NOVEMBER · DECEMBER

PAUSA · MAGHA · PHALGUNA · CHAITRA · VAISHAKA · JYAISTHA · ASADHA · SRAVANA · BHADRA · ASVINA · KARTIKA · AGHAN

Vasant Panchami festival of spring and of Saraswati, goddess of learning

Local festivals are celebrated throughout the year in villages all over India

Holi festival of spring and **Shivarati** dedicated to Shiva

Ramanavami the birth of Rama

Diwali festival of light and Hindu New Year

Dussehra (Ram Lila or Durga Puja) celebrates the triumph of good over evil

Ganesh Chaturthi dedicated to Ganesh

Raksha Bandhan festival of protection **Janmashtami** the birth of Krishna

Rath Yatra dedicated to Lord Jagannath, one of the names for Krishna

HOW TO MAKE A RAKHI BRACELET

The festival of Raksha Bandhan takes place on the day of the Full Moon in the month of Sravana (July-August). Girls tie bracelets, called *rakhis*, around their brothers' wrists for protection. In return, brothers give their sisters gifts, usually of money. Try making your own rakhi bracelets.

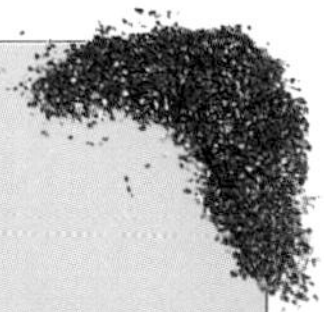

YOU WILL NEED:

- glue
- card
- tinsel
- ribbon or thick thread
- coloured glitter, sequins or small beads
- large coin
- scissors

WHAT TO DO:

1 Cut a small circle out of the card. Trace round a coin to get the right shape.

2 Cut a piece of ribbon or thick plaited thread to make the bracelet. Make sure the ribbon or thread is big enough to go around your wrist.

3 Glue the ribbon or thread across the back of the card circle.

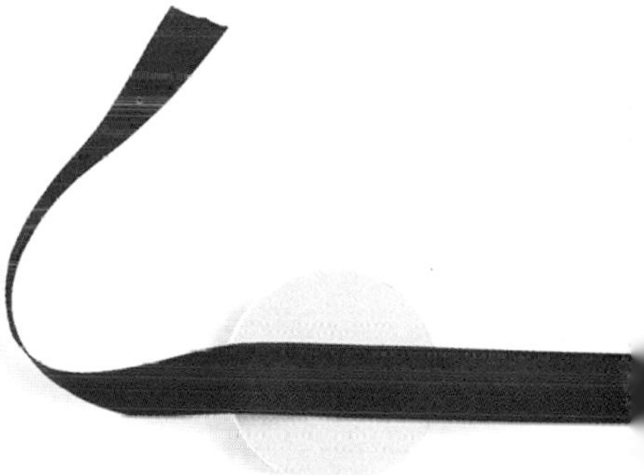

4 Decorate the card circle with tinsel, glitter or sequins. Or you can stick on tiny beads.

FAMILY CELEBRATIONS

The priest casts a horoscope at the time of a baby's birth. It will be consulted later to fix a good wedding date.

The family is very important to Hindus. In India, several generations of a family often live together in the same house and help to look after each other. For Hindus who have settled abroad, family ties and celebrations remain very important. There are many special celebrations in a Hindu's life. These are usually a time for the whole family to get together.

CELEBRATING A BIRTH

When a baby is born, a priest performs a special ceremony and says prayers for the good health and well-being of the mother and the baby. Ten days after the baby's birth, a naming ceremony takes place and the baby's horoscope is cast, showing the positions of the stars and planets at the time of its birth.

THE SACRED THREAD

For boys from the top three castes, the most important ceremony of their childhood takes place when they are between nine and eleven years old. This is when they receive their sacred thread from the priest.

They must wear these throughout their lives, looped over the left shoulder and under the right arm. This marks a new stage in a boy's life, when he begins to find out more about his religion and to take on more responsibility.

The priest prepares a young Hindu boy for his sacred thread ceremony, one of the most important times in his life.

DEATH AND CREMATION

When Hindus die, their bodies are cremated. In India, the body is placed on a pile of sandalwood logs which is set alight by the eldest son or eldest male relation. In other countries, the ceremony takes place in a crematorium. It is followed by 12 days of rites and rituals for the dead person's soul. If possible, the dead person's ashes are sprinkled into the water of the River Ganges.

Hindus believe that when you are cremated, your body perishes in the fire but your soul lives on to be born again.

It takes a bride several hours to put on her wedding sari, make-up and jewellery. Luckily, she has many willing helpers.

WEDDING DAY

Many Hindu weddings are arranged by the bride's and groom's parents. The wedding itself lasts for several days, with many rituals and ceremonies. The wedding can take place anywhere - at the bride's home, or in a special hall hired for the occasion. The bride wears special jewellery and a red silk sari. She sits with the groom in front of the sacred fire while the priest recites prayers and offers food to the gods. Then the bride and groom walk seven times around the fire to symbolise their marriage. After her wedding, the bride goes to live with her husband and his family.

Before her wedding, a bride's hands and feet are decorated with red mehndi patterns. The leaves of the mehndi, or henna, plant are crushed to form a paste and painted onto the bride's skin. After a few hours, the dried paste is washed off, leaving the pattern behind.

A bride-to-be is having her hands decorated with mehndi for her wedding. It takes a lot of patience and skill.

MEHNDI HANDS

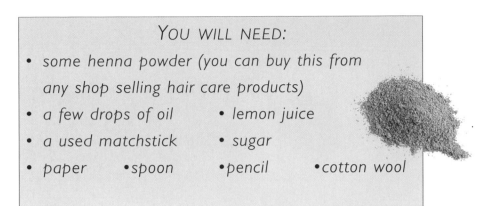

YOU WILL NEED:

- some henna powder (you can buy this from any shop selling hair care products)
- a few drops of oil   • lemon juice
- a used matchstick   • sugar
- paper   •spoon   •pencil   •cotton wool

WHAT TO DO:

1 First, sketch out your pattern on a piece of paper. Try lots of different patterns. Then dab your friend's hand with lemon juice and sugar on cotton wool. This is to make the mixture stick.

2 Mix some of the henna powder with the oil and lemon juice to form a thick paste.

4 Leave the paste to dry for 2-3 hours then scrape it off carefully. The pattern will last for several days.

3 Then use the matchstick and henna paste to draw the pattern on.

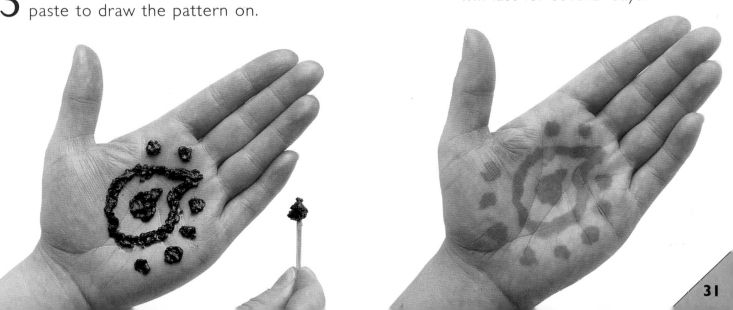

GLOSSARY

Aryans people from Central Asia who invaded north-west India in c.1,500 BC. Their religion laid the foundations for Hinduism.

Brahman the supreme spirit of Hinduism.

caste a large group, or class, of people. In Hindu society, there are four main castes.

cremation the ritual of burning the body to ashes after a person has died.

divinity a god or goddess.

eternity for ever.

halva a sweet dish made with nuts or carrots and eaten during many Hindu celebrations and festivals.

horoscope a chart drawn up to show the position of the stars and planets at the time of a person's birth and used for predicting a person's future life.

incense sweet-smelling fragrance burned in temples.

karma your actions and their effects.

moksha ultimate freedom or salvation from samsara. Being at one with Brahman.

pilgrimage a journey to an important religious place to pray or give thanks.

puja a common form of Hindu worship.

Ramayana one of the most sacred Hindu texts; tells the story of the god, Rama, and his wife, Sita.

reincarnation the belief that a person's soul is reborn into a different body when that person dies.

Rig Veda the oldest and one of the holiest Hindu texts.

Sanskrit the ancient, sacred language of Hinduism.

sari a style of dress worn by Indian women.

shrine part of a temple or a place of worship in a home, village or field.

samsara the cycle of birth, death and rebirth central to Hindu beliefs.

INDEX

Agni 5
Allahabad 23
Aryans 4-5, 18
ashrams 7

beginnings of Hinduism 4-5
beliefs 6-7
birth celebrations 28
bracelet (rakhi) 27
Brahma 10
Brahman 7, 10
Brahmins 7, 16

carrot halva (recipe) 9
caste system 7
cremation 29

Diwali 25
Durga 12, 25
Dussehra 25

elephant mask 13

family celebrations 29-9
festivals 8, 23, 24-5, 26

Ganesh 12, 26
Ganges 23, 29
gods and goddesses 10-12, 14

Hindu communities 5
Hindu New Year 26
Hinduism 4, 5, 6

Holi 24
holy men (sadhus) 16
holy places 22-3
horoscopes 28

karma 6
Krishna 11, 19, 20, 21, 26
Kshatriyas 7
Kumbh Mela fair 23

Lakshmi 10, 25
lamps (divas) 25

Mahabharata (epic poem) 19
marigold garland 17
meditation 16
mehndi (henna) hands 30,31
moksha (salvation) 7
Mount Kailash 23

offerings to the gods 15

Parvati 11, 12, 23
pilgrimages (yatras) 22, 23
prayers (puja) 14, 15, 24
priests 15, 16, 28, 29
Puranas (Sanskrit verses)19

Raksha Bandhan 27
Ram Lila 25
Rama 11, 19, 25, 26
Ramayana (epic poem) 19

reincarnation (samsara) 6
Rig Veda 5, 18, 19

sacred cities (tirthas) 22
sacred cows 8
sacred texts 18-19
sacred threads 28-9
Sanskrit 18
Saraswati 10, 26
scheduled castes 7
serpent king 20-1
Shiva 4, 5, 10, 11, 12, 16, 22, 23, 26
shrines 6, 14
soul (atman) 7, 29
Sri Amarnath cave 23
Sudras 7

temple bells 15
temples 4, 5, 6, 14, 15, 16

Upanishads (sacred texts) 19

Vaishyas 7
Varanasi 22
Vedas (sacred texts) 19
vegetarian diet 8
Vishnu 10, 11, 16

weddings 18, 30

yoga 16